LE CORDON BLEU

HOME COLLECTION

·DESSERTS·

PERIPLUS
EDITIONS

contents

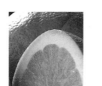

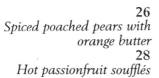

recipe ratings ❁ *easy* ❁❁ *a little more care needed* ❁❁❁ *more care needed*

Apple pie

When pilgrims first settled in North America, they took with them apple seeds and a love of pies, sowing a national love affair with this cherished homey dessert. Cooking apples yield the best results.

Preparation time **1 hour**
Total cooking time **1 hour**
Serves **4–6**

❀ ❀

PASTRY
2 cups all-purpose flour
2/3 cup unsalted butter, cubed
2 tablespoons sugar

FILLING
1 1/2 lb. large tart green apples
1/2 cup sugar, plus extra for sprinkling
1 teaspoon ground cinnamon
1/4 teaspoon ground nutmeg
3 tablespoons all-purpose flour
1 tablespoon lemon juice
3 tablespoons unsalted butter, cubed

1 Preheat the oven to 350°F. To make the pastry, work together the flour, butter, sugar and a pinch of salt in a food processor until the mixture resembles fine bread crumbs. With the motor running, add 2 tablespoons iced water and process until the mixture just comes together. Remove the dough, divide in half and flatten each portion into a thick disk. Cover with plastic wrap and chill in the refrigerator for 15–20 minutes.

2 To make the filling, peel, quarter and core the apples, then slice thinly and place in a large bowl. Combine the sugar, cinnamon, nutmeg, flour and a good pinch of salt, and sprinkle the mixture over the apple. Add the lemon juice and toss well.

3 On a lightly floured surface, roll out a pastry disk 1/8 inch thick, and 2 inches wider than a greased, shallow 9-inch pie plate. Carefully roll the dough onto a rolling pin, or fold into quarters, then ease into the pie plate. With your fingertips, press the dough into the plate to remove any air bubbles. Using a sharp, floured knife, trim the excess pastry, leaving a 1-inch border of dough overhanging the rim.

4 Add the filling, then with a pastry brush, brush the pastry edges with water. Roll the remaining dough to the same thickness as before. Dot the apple with butter, place the dough on top and cut four steam vents. Trim the excess pastry, leaving a 1/2-inch overhang, then press the edges together to seal them. Flute the edges by pinching the pastry between thumb and index finger into a zigzag design. Brush the top with water and sprinkle with extra sugar, then bake for 55–60 minutes. Cool the pie on a rack, and serve warm or cold.

Crème brûlée

The literal translation of this rich dessert is "burnt cream." Just before serving, chilled custard is sprinkled with sugar, which is quickly caramelized under a broiler to form a brittle topping, creating a delicious contrast in flavor and texture to the smooth, creamy custard beneath.

*Preparation time **20 minutes + overnight refrigeration***
*Total cooking time **55 minutes***
Serves 6

4 egg yolks
7 tablespoons sugar
2¹/₂ cups whipping cream
vanilla extract

1 Preheat the oven to 300°F. Have ready six ¹/₂-cup soufflé dishes or custard cups.
2 Whisk the egg yolks and 3 tablespoons sugar in a large heatproof bowl. Set aside. Bring the cream and a few drops of vanilla to a boil in a heavy-bottomed saucepan, then reduce the heat and simmer for about 8 minutes. Remove the pan from the heat and slowly pour the cream onto the egg mixture, whisking vigorously so the eggs do not scramble. Strain the custard into a large pitcher, then pour into the individual soufflé dishes.
3 Place the soufflé dishes in a baking dish. Pour enough hot water into the baking dish to reach ¹/₂ inch below the rims of the soufflé dishes. Bake the custard for 40–45 minutes, or until just firm to the touch. Remove from the oven, allow to cool, then cover and refrigerate overnight.
4 To make the caramel, evenly sprinkle some of the remaining 4 tablespoons of sugar over the top of each custard using a teaspoon. Without breaking the skin of the custard, spread the sugar out very gently using a finger or the spoon, then repeat to form a second layer of sugar. Remove any sugar from the inside edges of the dishes as it will burn. Place the dishes on a baking sheet and place under a very hot broiler for 2–3 minutes, or until the sugar has melted and is just beginning to give off a haze. Allow the glaze to harden before serving.

Chef's tips This wonderful dessert is enhanced by fruit, which complement the sweetness of the custard with a fresh tangy flavor. Before pouring the custard into the soufflé dishes, arrange a few berries (strawberries or raspberries are ideal) in the bottom of the dish, or prunes presoaked in Armagnac or brandy.

Hot Cointreau and orange soufflé

A beautifully risen, hot soufflé is always a sight to behold. This spectacular dessert, flavored simply with the sweetness of sun-drenched orange, will create a sensation among even the most discerning dinner guests.

Preparation time **35 minutes**
Total cooking time **20 minutes**
Serves 6

softened butter, for coating
1/3 cup sugar, for coating
2 tablespoons orange juice
2 teaspoons grated orange rind
1 tablespoon Cointreau
1 cup milk
1/2 vanilla bean, split lengthwise
4 eggs, separated
1 tablespoon all-purpose flour
1 tablespoon cornstarch
sifted confectioners' sugar, for dusting

1 Preheat the oven to 350°F. Using a pastry brush, brush the insides of six 1/2-cup soufflé dishes with softened butter, working the brush from the bottom upwards. Refrigerate to set and repeat.

2 Half-fill a soufflé dish with sugar, and without placing your fingers inside the dish, rotate it so that a layer of sugar adheres to the butter. Tap out the excess sugar and repeat with the remaining soufflé dishes.

3 Place the orange juice and grated rind in a small saucepan over medium-high heat. Simmer for 3–5 minutes to reduce the volume by three-quarters—the mixture should be quite syrupy. Pour in the Cointreau, scraping the base of the pan with a wooden spoon. Remove from the heat and allow to cool.

4 Bring the milk and vanilla bean slowly to a boil. In a bowl, and using a wooden spoon, mix together 1/4 cup of the sugar and two of the egg yolks, then mix in the flour and cornstarch. Remove the vanilla bean from the boiling milk; stir a little of the milk into the egg mixture, then add all the mixture to the milk in the pan. Stir rapidly with the wooden spoon over medium heat until the mixture thickens and comes to a boil. Then boil gently for 1 minute to cook the flour, stirring constantly to prevent sticking.

5 Pour the mixture into a clean bowl, stir to cool it slightly, then beat in the reduced orange sauce. Stir in the remaining two egg yolks and dab a small piece of butter over the surface to melt and prevent a skin forming. (If you prefer, place a sheet of parchment paper on the surface instead.)

6 In a clean, dry bowl, whisk the egg whites until they form soft peaks. Add the remaining sugar and whisk for 30 seconds. Add a third of the egg whites to the custard and lightly beat in until just combined. Using a large metal spoon, fold in the remaining egg whites gently but quickly. Do not overmix, as this will cause the mixture to lose volume and become heavy.

7 Place the soufflé dishes on a baking sheet. Spoon in the mixture to completely fill each dish, smooth the surface of each soufflé and sprinkle with sifted confectioners' sugar. Roll your thumb around the inside of each dish to create a ridge that will enable the soufflé to rise evenly (see Chef's techniques, page 63). Bake for 12 minutes, or until well risen with a light crust. The soufflés should feel just set when pressed lightly with a fingertip. Serve at once.

Chef's tip This soufflé—to the end of step 4—can be prepared a few hours in advance.

Molded fruit terrine

This luscious dessert yields a truly fruit-filled flavor with every tingling mouthful.
The secret is to use two loaf pans instead of one, sitting one on top of the other to
prevent the fruit from floating to the top before the gelatin has set.

Preparation time **40 minutes + 1–2 nights refrigeration**
Total cooking time **5–10 minutes**
Serves 8

¹/2 cup black currants
³/4 cup red currants
³/4 cup blueberries
1³/4 cups strawberries
3 cups raspberries
4 leaves gelatin or 2 teaspoons gelatin powder
I cup rosé wine
2 tablespoons sugar
I tablespoon lemon juice
¹/4 cup strained raspberry purée
  (see Chef's tips)

1 Pick through all the fruit and remove any stalks, then gently mix the fruit together, taking care not to bruise or damage any. Soak the gelatin leaves or powder, following the Chef's techniques on page 63.
2 Carefully arrange the fruit into a loaf pan measuring 9 x 5 x 3 inches, placing the smaller fruits on the bottom.

3 In a small saucepan, heat half the wine until it begins to simmer. Remove the pan from the heat and add the sugar, gelatin and lemon juice. Stir to dissolve. Add the remaining wine and the raspberry purée. Reserve ²/3 cup of the liquid and pour the rest over the fruit. Cover with plastic wrap. Place a lightly weighted 9-inch loaf pan on top, then refrigerate for at least 1 hour, or overnight if possible, until the mold has set. Remove the top loaf pan and plastic wrap.
4 Gently warm the reserved wine mixture and pour over the surface of the mold. Cover again with plastic wrap and refrigerate overnight to set.
5 Just before serving, turn out the mold by dipping the base of the pan very briefly in hot water and inverting it onto a plate. Slice the terrine, decorate with some extra fresh berries, and serve with crème fraîche.

Chef's tips Straining about 1¹/4 cups of raspberries will produce the required quantity of raspberry purée.

  Do not rinse the raspberries, and only rinse the other fruit if it is sandy.

  Small strawberries give the best results in this fruit terrine, but if they are not available, you could use larger strawberries, cut in half.

Pink grapefruit sorbet

This sublime sorbet may be served in a tall glass as a refreshing dessert, or in a sherry glass as a palate cleanser. For best results, use an ice-cream maker.

Preparation time **30 minutes + churning or beating + freezing**
Total cooking time **1 minute**
Serves 6

3/4 cup sugar
3/4 cup pink or yellow grapefruit juice (about 3 grapefruit)
1/3 cup lemon juice
1 cup dry white wine
1/3 cup Campari
6 sprigs of lemon balm or mint, to garnish

1 Stir the sugar and 2/3 cup water in a medium saucepan over low heat until the sugar dissolves. Bring to a boil, and allow to boil for 1 minute. Remove from the heat and leave to cool.

2 Combine the grapefruit and lemon juice and strain into a pitcher. Add the wine, Campari and cooled syrup.

3 Churn in an ice-cream maker for 30–40 minutes, or until thick and slushy, then transfer to a stainless steel container. Cover well with plastic wrap, then foil, and freeze for 1 hour before use.

4 Alternatively, freeze the mixture in a stainless steel container for about 3 hours, or until firm. Scoop into a large bowl and beat with an electric mixer for 1–2 minutes, or until thick and creamy. Return the mixture to the container and freeze for 3 hours. Repeat the beating and freezing twice, then freeze overnight.

5 Remove from the freezer and refrigerate for about 20 minutes before serving. Scoop the mixture into well-chilled glasses and decorate each with a sprig of lemon balm or mint.

Chef's tip This sorbet can be frozen for up to 3 months.

Twice-baked chocolate cakes

*These dark, fudgy cakes are sinfully rich and totally irresistible, with a dense base and a soufflé-like
top that rises beautifully with the help of a paper collar. Sheer indulgence!*

*Preparation time **1 hour 25 minutes***
*Total cooking time **35 minutes***
Serves 6

6 oz. semi-sweet cooking chocolate
2/3 cup unsalted butter
4 tablespoons cocoa powder
6 eggs, separated
1/2 cup sugar
cocoa and confectioners' sugar, to dust

1 Preheat the oven to 325°F. Lightly grease six baking rings, each 3 inches across and 3/4 inch tall. Line a baking sheet with parchment paper, grease the paper and set the baking rings on the baking sheet.
2 Cut six strips of parchment paper, each one 12 x 41/2 inches. Make a 1/2 inch fold along one long edge of each strip, then make 1/2 inch diagonal cuts up to the fold, spaced about 1/4 inch apart. Line the rings with the strips of paper so that the diagonal cuts sit very flat on the base of the baking sheet. Press out any air bubbles with a pastry brush and refrigerate until ready to fill.
3 Melt the chocolate in the top of a double boiler over a pan of simmering water. Add the butter and cocoa

powder, whisk until smooth, and set aside.
4 Whisk the egg whites in a clean, dry bowl until stiff peaks form, then gradually beat in half the sugar until smooth and glossy. In a separate bowl, beat together the egg yolks and the remaining sugar for 5 minutes, or until light in color and a ribbon forms when the whisk is lifted out of the bowl. Gently fold in the egg whites using a rubber spatula or large metal spoon. Gently fold in the chocolate mixture.
5 Divide half the mixture evenly among the rings, being careful not to get batter on the paper above. Bake for 15 minutes, then remove and cool completely. (The cakes will collapse and flatten.) Spoon the remaining mixture into each ring, covering the cake. Bake for 15–20 minutes. When cooked, the center of the top of the cakes will stay steady when the tray is gently jiggled.
6 Slide a thin metal spatula under each ring and carefully loosen the cakes from the baking sheet. Remove the rings, carefully peel the paper sleeves from the cakes and place on a serving plate. Dust with a little combined cocoa and confectioners' sugar. Serve at once.

Chef's tip Filling the rings with cake mixture is most easily done using a pastry bag fitted with a medium plain nozzle.

Thin apple tart

This spectacular tart—Tarte fine aux pommes—has a crisp sweet short pastry base spread with almond cream and topped with glazed apples. This recipe calls for Golden Delicious apples, but you can use any apple that holds its shape when cooked.

Preparation time 1 hour + 40 minutes refrigeration
Total cooking time 1 hour
Serves 6–8

PASTRY
I cup all-purpose flour
1/3 cup confectioner's sugar
3 tablespoons unsalted butter
I egg yolk
vanilla extract

ALMOND CREAM
1/4 cup confectioners' sugar
2 tablespoons unsalted butter, softened
I teaspoon vanilla extract
I egg yolk
1/4 cup ground almonds

I lb. Golden Delicious apples,
   or similar variety (about 2–3)
juice of I lemon
apricot jam, for glazing

1 To make the pastry, sift the flour and confectioners' sugar into a bowl, then cut in the butter until the mixture resembles bread crumbs. Make a well in the center and add the egg yolk, a few drops of vanilla, a pinch of salt and enough cold water to help form a dough. Turn out onto a lightly floured surface and gather the dough together to make a smooth ball. Cover with plastic wrap and refrigerate for 30 minutes, or until just firm.

2 Preheat the oven to 350°F. Remove the plastic wrap from the chilled pastry, then very gently roll out the pastry between two sheets of waxed paper to a thickness of 1/8 inch. Carefully ease the pastry into a greased, 9-inch fluted tart pan with removable base.

3 Bake the unfilled shell for 20 minutes, following the Chef's techniques on page 62. Remove the rice or baking beans and paper, then bake for another 10 minutes, covering the pastry with foil if the pastry looks as though it might burn. Remove from the oven and allow to cool.

4 To make the almond cream, beat together the confectioners' sugar, butter and vanilla until light and creamy. Add the egg yolk and beat well, then add the ground almonds. Spread the mixture in an even layer over the cooled pastry shell.

5 Peel, quarter and core the apples, then sprinkle them with lemon juice. Thinly slice the apples and arrange in overlapping circles over the layer of almond cream. Bake for 20–25 minutes, or until the apples are cooked. Place on a wire rack to cool.

6 When the tart has cooled, place some apricot jam in a small saucepan and bring to a boil. (Add a spoonful of water if the jam becomes too thick for spreading.) Strain the jam and, using a pastry brush, lightly dab the surface of the tart with the jam—this will give the apples a nice shine and prevent them from drying out.

Chef's tips Handle the pastry as little as possible, and work quickly and lightly.

Cool the tart before brushing it with the apricot jam. If the tart is still hot, the fruit will simply soak up the jam and the tart will lose its shine when it cools.

Vanilla ice cream

*No commercial ice cream can ever compare with the creamy, decadent
richness of the homemade variety. This classic favorite is peppered with fine black specks:
the tiny seeds of the vanilla bean, which release a fabulous flavor. For a light, smooth
result every time, with minimal fuss, an ice-cream machine is highly recommended.*

*Preparation time **20 minutes + churning or beating
+ freezing***
*Total cooking time **10 minutes***
Serves 4

5 egg yolks
1/3 cup sugar
1 1/2 cups milk
1 vanilla bean, split lengthwise
1/2 cup heavy cream

1 Whisk the egg yolks and sugar in the top of a double
boiler until thick and creamy and almost white. Bring
the milk and vanilla bean slowly to a boil in a heavy-
bottomed saucepan. Gradually whisk the boiling milk
into the eggs and sugar, then transfer the mixture to a
clean pan. Stir constantly with a wooden spoon over low
heat for about 3–5 minutes, or until the custard thickly
coats the back of the spoon. Ensure that the mixture
does not boil, as this will cause it to separate.

2 Pour through a fine strainer into a clean bowl.
Place the bowl in some iced water to cool. When the
custard is very cold, stir in the cream, then pour the
mixture into an ice-cream machine and churn for
10–20 minutes, or until the paddle leaves a trail in the
ice cream, or the ice cream holds its own shape. Remove
from the machine and freeze in an airtight, stainless
steel container for 3–4 hours or overnight.

3 Alternatively, freeze the custard and cream mixture
in a 1-quart container for 3 hours, or until firm. Scoop
into a large bowl and beat with an electric mixer for
1–2 minutes, or until thick and creamy. Return the
mixture to the container and freeze for 3 hours. Repeat
the beating and freezing twice, then freeze overnight.

Chef's tip This ice cream can take on a range of flavors.
A little coffee extract may be added to the custard at
the end of step 1, or 1/3–2/3 cup chopped chocolate may
be added to the milk before boiling. Another delicious
option is to fold amaretto liqueur or crushed biscuits
into the frozen ice cream before it is stored.

Shortbread cookies with fresh cream and fruit

This easy-to-assemble dessert is a wicked union of sweet red fruit and luscious whipped cream, anchored in rounds of lemon-tinged shortbread cookies.

*Preparation time **45 minutes + refrigeration***
*Total cooking time **20–25 minutes***
*Serves **4–6***

SHORTBREAD COOKIES
1 1/4 cups unsalted butter, softened
1 1/4 cups confectioners' sugar
finely grated rind of 1 lemon
vanilla extract
1 egg, lightly beaten
3 1/2 cups all-purpose flour, sifted

FILLING
3/4 cup whipping cream
1 teaspoon vanilla extract
sugar, to taste
1 cup assorted red berries, such as strawberries, raspberries and red currants

confectioners' sugar, for dusting
fresh mint leaves, to garnish

1 Brush two baking sheets with melted butter and refrigerate. Preheat the oven to 325°F. To make the pastry, beat the butter and confectioners' sugar until pale and creamy. Stir in the rind and a few drops of vanilla. Add the egg gradually, beating well after each addition. Add the flour in one batch and stir until combined: the mixture will be very soft and sticky.

2 Divide the mixture in half. Roll out each portion 1/8 inch thick between two layers of well-floured waxed paper, working quickly and lightly. Place on the chilled baking sheets with the paper still attached, then refrigerate until firm.

3 Slide the pastry off the baking sheets onto a work surface. Remove the top piece of paper, dip a 3 1/2-inch fluted cookie-cutter in flour and cut out cookies. Ease the cookies off the bottom sheet of paper onto the buttered baking sheets and pierce with a fork. Bake for 20–25 minutes, or until golden; allow to cool briefly on the baking sheets before cooling on a rack.

4 To make the filling, pour the cream into a bowl, add the vanilla and sugar to taste. Whisk into soft peaks. Spoon into a pastry bag fitted with an 8-cut star nozzle.

5 To assemble, pipe some cream onto the center of a cookie; arrange some fruit around the cream (but not over the edge). Top with a second cookie, repeat the fruit and cream, then top with a third cookie, dusted with confectioners' sugar. Finish the remaining stacks, reserving some fruit. Transfer to serving plates and decorate with mint and reserved fruit.

Chocolate and Cointreau mousse

Mousse in French literally means froth or foam. This melt-in-the-mouth mousse marries the classic flavors of chocolate and orange, is simple to prepare, and makes a magical finale to any meal.

*Preparation time **40 minutes + 1 hour refrigeration***
*Total cooking time **5 minutes***
Serves 4–6

4 oz. semi-sweet cooking chocolate
3 tablespoons unsalted butter
1/4 cup orange juice
3 tablespoons cocoa powder
2 eggs, separated
2 tablespoons Cointreau
1/3 cup whipping cream
1 egg white
2 tablespoons sugar
orange segments and whipped cream, to serve

1 Place the chocolate, butter and orange juice in the top of a double boiler over a pan of barely simmering water. When the chocolate and butter have melted, stir in the cocoa powder. Remove from the water and whisk in the egg yolks and Cointreau. Leave to cool.

2 In a chilled bowl, beat the cream until soft peaks form. Cover and refrigerate until ready to use.

3 Beat all the egg whites in a clean, dry bowl until soft peaks form. Add the sugar; beat until smooth and glossy.

4 Using a large metal spoon, gently fold the egg whites into the cooled chocolate mixture. Before they are completely incorporated, fold in the whipped cream. Spoon the mixture into individual serving dishes or a large serving bowl and refrigerate for at least 1 hour. Serve with orange segments and whipped cream.

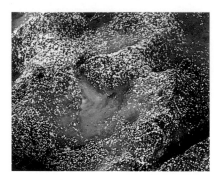

Bread pudding with panettone

When the yearning strikes for a homey dessert, bread pudding is hard to beat.
For special occasions, this humble and economical dish can be transformed into something really
marvelous with candied fruits, a dash of rum, some brioche or, as in this case, Italian panettone.

*Preparation time **20 minutes***
*Total cooking time **50 minutes***
Serves 4

¼ cup golden raisins
2 tablespoons rum, brandy or amaretto liqueur
8 oz. panettone
3 eggs
¼ cup sugar
2 cups milk
1 vanilla bean, split lengthwise
1 tablespoon smooth apricot jam, warmed
confectioners' sugar, for dusting

1 Preheat the oven to 325°F. Place the raisins in a 9-inch oval baking dish or casserole and pour the alcohol over the top.
2 Cut the panettone horizontally to make two or three round slices about ½ inch thick, then remove the crust.

Cut each slice into quarters (almost triangles). Neatly overlap them in the base of the dish.
3 Lightly whisk the eggs and sugar in a heatproof bowl until just combined. Place the milk and vanilla bean in a saucepan, bring to a boil, then slowly pour the scalded milk into the egg and sugar mixture, whisking constantly.
4 Pour the mixture through a fine sieve into the dish, over the panettone. Place the dish in a larger baking dish half full of hot water. Bake for 40–45 minutes, or until the custard has set and is golden brown. Remove the pudding from the oven and, while still warm, brush the surface with the warm apricot jam. Sprinkle with confectioners' sugar and serve either hot or cold.

Chef's tips If the panettone is not sweet, add some sugar to taste.
  Raisin loaf is a perfect alternative to panettone as it already has a loaf shape. Simply cut off the crusts, slice the bread and cut each slice in half to form triangles.

Spiced poached pears with orange butter

In this simply elegant dessert, the pears are gently infused with the flavors of real vanilla and star anise, then fringed with wisps of glazed peel, and served with a Cointreau-laced orange sauce.

*Preparation time **1 hour***
*Total cooking time **1 hour***
Serves 4

✤ ✤

I lemon
1¹/2 lb. oranges (about 5)
2³/4 cups sugar
I vanilla bean, split lengthwise
3 sticks cinnamon
10 whole black peppercorns
4 star anise
3 whole cloves
pinch of nutmeg
6 pears, about 3 lb.
fresh mint leaves, to garnish

ORANGE BUTTER
1¹/2 cups orange juice
¹/2 cup unsalted butter, cut into cubes
2 tablespoons Cointreau

1 Peel the rind off the lemon and one orange with a vegetable peeler, without scraping the bitter white pith. Place the rind in a large saucepan with 2 quarts water and 2 cups of the sugar. Wrap the whole spices in cheesecloth for easy removal later, and add them to the pan with the nutmeg. Stir over a low heat until the sugar dissolves, then bring to a gentle simmer.
2 Peel the pears, leaving the stems intact, and add them to the simmering liquid. Allow them to simmer gently for 20 minutes, or until easily pierced with a knife tip. They should be just tender, but not soft. Remove from the heat and allow to cool in the liquid.

3 To make the orange butter, bring the orange juice to a boil in a small saucepan, reduce the heat and simmer for 30 minutes, or until reduced by three-quarters. Remove from the heat and whisk in the butter, a few pieces at a time. Whisk in the Cointreau and set aside.
4 Peel the rind from the remaining oranges, avoiding the bitter white pith. Cut the rind into thin strips and set aside. Cut the tops and bottoms off the oranges and discard. Place the oranges on a cutting board and with a sharp knife, cut from top to bottom, following the curve of the fruit to expose the flesh. Cut between the membranes to remove the orange segments. Set aside.
5 Place the strips of orange rind in a small saucepan and cover with water. Bring to a boil, strain the rind and rinse with cold water. Return to the pan with ¹/3 cup water and the remaining sugar. Stir over low heat to dissolve the sugar, then bring to a boil. Reduce the heat and leave the rinds to slowly simmer in the syrup for 20 minutes—they will become translucent. Strain over a bowl, reserving the liquid. Add the liquid to the orange butter, and cool the rinds on a piece of parchment paper.
6 Remove two of the cooled pears and cut them in half. Remove the cores and stems, then slice the pear halves thinly. Place a sliced half on each plate, as well as a whole pear. Drizzle the orange butter around and arrange some glazed rind on top of the pear slices. Decorate with the orange segments and fresh mint.

Chef's tips Poached pears will improve in flavor and texture if prepared 1 or 2 days in advance. They can be refrigerated for up to 1 week in the syrup.

Star anise pods, shown opposite, are available from Asian food markets and some supermarkets.

Hot passionfruit soufflés

Feather-light, these wonderful soufflés tantalize the tastebuds with the tart sweetness and tropical perfume of passionfruit.

*Preparation time **20 minutes***
*Total cooking time **20 minutes***
Serves 4

softened unsalted butter, for coating
sugar, for coating
1/2 cup sugar
12 passionfruit or 1/2 cup passionfruit pulp
6 egg whites
confectioners' sugar, for dusting

1 Prepare four 1-cup ramekins or individual soufflé dishes or custard cups by brushing the inside of each with softened butter, using a pastry brush. Refrigerate the dishes until the butter is firm, then brush on another layer of butter and chill again. Half-fill one of the dishes with sugar, and without placing your fingers inside the dish, rotate it so that a layer of sugar adheres to the butter. Tap out the excess sugar and use it to coat the other dishes.

2 Preheat the oven to 325°F. Pass the passionfruit pulp through a strainer into a bowl and add 1/4 cup of the sugar. Discard the seeds.

3 Whisk the egg whites until soft peaks form. Sprinkle the remaining sugar onto the egg whites and whisk for 1 minute. Gently fold the egg whites into the passionfruit pulp. Spoon a quarter of the mixture into each soufflé dish and smooth the surface. Sprinkle the top of each soufflé with sifted confectioners' sugar, then run your thumb around the inside of the dish to create a ridge so the soufflés rise evenly (see Chef's techniques, page 63).

4 Place the soufflé dishes in a baking dish, and pour in enough hot water to reach halfway up the soufflé dishes. Bake for 20 minutes, or until well risen. Once baked, sprinkle with more sifted confectioners' sugar and serve the soufflés immediately.

Creamed rice pudding

Whipped cream makes this rice pudding extravagantly rich and creamy.
A sharp fruit sauce or compote is the perfect accompaniment.

*Preparation time **10 minutes***
*Total cooking time **30 minutes***
Serves 4–6

¼ cup short-grain rice
2½ cups milk
1 vanilla bean, split lengthwise
3 tablespoons sugar
⅔ cup whipping cream

1 Place the rice in a strainer and rinse thoroughly under running water until the water runs clear. Drain.
2 Pour the milk into a medium heavy-bottomed saucepan, add the vanilla bean and rice, then bring slowly to a boil. Reduce the heat and gently simmer, stirring frequently, for about 30 minutes, or until the rice is soft and creamy. When a spoon is drawn across the base of the pan, a clear parting in the rice should be left behind.
3 Stir in the sugar and transfer the mixture to a large bowl. Remove the vanilla bean, cover the surface with plastic wrap and allow to cool. Lightly whip the cream in a separate bowl until soft peaks form. When the pudding is cold, carefully fold in the cream. Serve with a fruit sauce or compote.

Chef's tip Because this dessert is so rich, you may choose to add only half of the whipped cream.

If you want to vary the flavor of this dessert, try adding a small pinch of powdered cinnamon or nutmeg with the sugar.

Apple strudel

In Vienna it is said that in the making of a perfect apple strudel, the dough is stretched so finely that a love letter may be read through it.

*Preparation time **40 minutes + 30 minutes resting***
*Total cooking time **50 minutes***
Serves 6–8

❁ ❁ ❁

1¹/2 cups bread flour or all-purpose flour
1 egg, lightly beaten
¹/2 cup unsalted butter
1 cup fresh bread crumbs
¹/4 cup sugar
2 teaspoons ground cinnamon
1¹/4 lb. cooking or very tart dessert apples
   (about 4 medium)
¹/2 cup golden raisins
confectioners' sugar, for dusting

1 Sift the flour and a pinch of salt into a large bowl. Make a well in the center, add the beaten egg and ¹/4 cup warm water, and mix with your hands to a smooth dough. With the bowl tipped to one side, and with open fingers, beat the dough, rotating your wrist. The dough is ready when it pulls away from the bowl and is difficult to beat. Place in a clean, lightly floured bowl, cover and leave in a warm place for 15 minutes.

2 Melt half of the butter in a skillet. Slowly fry the bread crumbs until golden brown, then set aside to cool in a bowl. Mix the sugar and cinnamon in a small bowl. Preheat the oven to 350°F.

3 Thoroughly flour one side of a large clean dish towel, place the pastry on top and, with your fingers, gently stretch the dough to a large rectangle about 24 x 20 inches; cover with another dish towel and set aside for 15 minutes. Melt the remaining butter and set aside.

4 Peel, quarter, core and thinly slice the apples, and combine with the bread crumbs, cinnamon mixture and raisins. Brush the dough liberally with the melted butter, then sprinkle the apple mixture all over the dough. Trim away the thick edge with a pair of scissors.

5 Pick up the dish towel from the shorter side, and push away and down from you to lightly roll the strudel up like a jelly roll. Tip the strudel carefully onto a baking sheet, seam-side-down or to one side. Leave the strudel straight, or curve it lightly into the traditional crescent. Brush the pastry with any remaining butter.

6 Bake for 35–45 minutes, or until crisp and golden. Cool slightly, sprinkle with confectioners' sugar and serve warm with vanilla custard, ice cream or whipped cream served alongside.

Clafouti

This classic dessert is based on a dish originating in the French country region of Limousin, where clafouti is enjoyed when sweet, dark cherries are ripe. Cherries are the favored fruit for this dessert, although plums or pears may also be used.

Preparation time **40 minutes**
Total cooking time **45 minutes**
Serves 4

**1 fresh peach or 2 canned peach halves,
   drained of syrup**
8 oz. fresh cherries
2 cups heavy cream
1 vanilla bean, split lengthwise
6 egg yolks
1 egg
1 tablespoon custard powder
3 tablespoons all-purpose flour
2 tablespoons Cointreau
confectioners' sugar, for dusting

1 Preheat the oven to 300°F. If you are using a fresh peach, blanch it in boiling water for 10–20 seconds, then transfer to a bowl of iced water. Peel the peach and cut around the fruit towards the stone. Gently twist the halves in opposite directions to expose the stone, then lift out the stone with a knife. If the peach is too slippery, simply cut the flesh from the stone. Process or purée one peach half and measure out 3 tablespoons of purée. Slice the remaining peach half into neat segments and set aside. Pit the cherries and set aside.

2 Place the cream in a heavy-bottomed saucepan with the vanilla bean, then heat until scalding—this is when bubbles form around the edge of the cream surface, yet the cream is not boiling. Remove the vanilla bean.

3 Whisk the egg yolks and the whole egg together in a large bowl. Beat in the custard powder and flour, then stir in the peach purée. Whisk the scalded cream into the egg mixture. Add the Cointreau and stir.

4 Lightly grease a 2-quart shallow baking dish or casserole with softened butter. Place all the fruit in the dish. Pour the custard over and bake for about 40 minutes, or until a skewer inserted into the center of the dessert comes out clean. Remove from the oven and immediately sift the confectioners' sugar over the top. Serve warm.

Iced raspberry soufflé

This chilled raspberry soufflé always looks wonderful and is a great conversation piece. It can also be made days—if not weeks—ahead, leaving more time for you to spend with your guests.

*Preparation time **45 minutes + 6 hours freezing
+ 30 minutes standing***
*Total cooking time **10 minutes***
*Serves **4–6***

🕯 🕯

2¹/4 cups raspberries
I cup sugar
5 egg whites
2¹/4 cups whipping cream
fresh raspberries, to garnish
sprigs of fresh mint, to garnish

1 Purée the raspberries in a food processor, then press through a fine sieve to eliminate the seeds. Measure out 1¹/4 cups of raspberry purée and set aside.
2 Cut out a piece of waxed paper to measure 10 x 3¹/2 inches. Wrap the paper around the outside of a 1-quart, 7-inch-diameter soufflé dish to make a collar. Secure the overlapping paper in place with tape or kitchen string, trying to keep the paper free of creases.

3 Place the sugar and ¹/4 cup water in a medium heavy-bottomed saucepan and heat gently to dissolve the sugar. Bring the syrup to a boil, then follow the Chef's techniques for making Italian meringue on page 63.
4 In a separate bowl, whip 1¹/2 cups of cream until they form soft peaks.
5 Using a metal spoon, gently fold the meringue into the reserved raspberry purée until thoroughly mixed, then fold in the cream until the streaks disappear. Be careful not to overmix, as this will cause the cream to thicken and separate and make the soufflé look grainy.
6 Spoon the mixture into the soufflé dish right up to the edge of the paper collar, then gently smooth the surface of the soufflé. Place in the freezer for a minimum of 6 hours. Just before serving, peel off the paper collar and allow the soufflé to stand for 30 minutes to soften. Whip the remaining ³/4 cup cream and use it to decorate the top of the soufflé. Finally, garnish the soufflé with the fresh raspberries and sprigs of mint.

Lemon tart with Italian meringue

This delicious shortcrust pastry case is smothered by a creamy lemon filling and a layer of satiny meringue. It should be baked and served on the same day.

*Preparation time **45 minutes + 40 minutes refrigeration***
*Total cooking time **45 minutes***
Serves 6

❋ ❋

PASTRY
1²/3 cups all-purpose flour, sifted
1 teaspoon sugar
1/3 cup unsalted butter, chopped
1 egg
1 teaspoon vanilla extract

LEMON FILLING
3 egg yolks
2/3 cup sugar
2 teaspoons finely grated lemon rind
juice of 3 lemons
2 tablespoons unsalted butter

3/4 cup sugar
4 egg whites
1 tablespoon confectioners' sugar, for dusting

1 To make the pastry, sift the flour, sugar and a good pinch of salt into a bowl. Cut in the butter until the mixture resembles fine bread crumbs. Make a well in the center. Combine the egg, vanilla and 2 teaspoons cold water and pour into the well. Slowly stir together with a flat-bladed knife, adding more flour if the mixture is slightly sticky. Gather the dough together to form a ball, wrap in plastic wrap and refrigerate for 20 minutes.

2 Preheat the oven to 350°F. Gently roll the pastry between two sheets of parchment paper to about 1/8 inch thick, then ease into a lightly greased, shallow 9-inch fluted tart pan with removable base. Bake the unfilled shell for 10 minutes, following the Chef's techniques on page 62. Remove the rice or baking beans and the paper. Bake for 10 more minutes, or until the center begins to color. Remove from the oven and cool on a wire rack.

3 To prepare the filling, whisk or beat the egg yolks and sugar in the top of a double boiler until light and creamy. Add the lemon rind, juice and then the butter. Place over a saucepan of barely simmering water and whisk constantly for 15–20 minutes, or until thickened. When ready, the mixture will leave a "ribbon" when drizzled from the whisk. While the filling is still hot, pour it into the cooled tart shell.

4 Place the 3/4 cup sugar and 3 tablespoons water in a medium heavy-bottomed saucepan and heat gently to dissolve the sugar. Bring to a boil, then follow the Chef's techniques for making Italian meringue on page 63.

5 Place the meringue in a pastry bag fitted with a 1/2-inch star nozzle. Starting in the center, pipe the meringue in continuous concentric circles covering the entire tart, keeping the meringue inside the pastry edge. Dust the surface with confectioners' sugar. Bake for 5 minutes, or until the meringue is lightly colored. Leave to cool and then refrigerate for 20 minutes, or until the filling is set.

Chef's tip If possible, refrigerate the dough overnight; it helps prevent the pastry from shrinking during baking.

Crêpes Suzette

*In this illustrious dessert, very fine pancakes are warmed in a lightly caramelized
orange butter sauce, then doused with Cointreau and ignited to flaming glory,
ending any repast on a note of unforgettable flourish.*

*Preparation time **30 minutes + 30 minutes resting***
*Total cooking time **45 minutes***
Makes 12 crêpes

CREPE BATTER
3/4 cup all-purpose flour
I teaspoon sugar
2 eggs, plus I egg yolk, lightly beaten
2/3 cup milk
2 tablespoons clarified butter, melted (see page 62)

clarified butter, for cooking (see page 62)

SAUCE
4 white sugar cubes
I 1/2 lb. oranges (about 5)
3 tablespoons clarified butter, melted (see page 62)
1/4 cup sugar
3 tablespoons Cointreau
2 tablespoons brandy

1 To make the batter, sift the flour into a bowl with a
pinch of salt and the sugar. Make a well in the center,
then add the eggs and extra egg yolk. Mix well with a
wooden spoon or whisk, gradually incorporating the
flour. Combine the milk with 1/4 cup water and
gradually add to the batter. Add the clarified butter and
beat until smooth. Cover and set aside for 30 minutes.

2 Melt a little clarified butter over medium heat in a
heavy-bottomed or nonstick 6-inch crêpe pan or skillet.
Pour off any excess butter, leaving a fine coating. Tilt the
pan and pour in a little batter, swirling the pan to create

a thin layer. Cook for 1–2 minutes, or until the edges are
light brown. Loosen the edges with a flat-bladed knife
or spatula and turn or flip the crêpe over. Cook for
about 1 minute, then turn onto a sheet of waxed paper
and cover with a dish towel. Repeat until all the batter
has been used up, each time lightly coating the skillet
with clarified butter.

3 To make the sauce, rub all the sugar cube sides over
the rind of an orange to soak up the oily zest, then crush
the cubes with the back of a wooden spoon. Squeeze
the oranges to produce 1 1/4 cups liquid. Over low heat,
melt the clarified butter in a wide shallow skillet or
sauté pan. Dissolve the crushed sugar in the butter, then
add the sugar. Cook, stirring, for 2 minutes. Slowly add
the orange juice, keeping well clear of the pan as the
mixture may spit. Increase the heat to medium and
simmer until reduced by a third.

4 Fold the crêpes in half, then into triangles. Place them
in the orange sauce, slightly overlapping, with their
points showing. Tilt the pan, scoop up the sauce and
pour it over the crêpes to moisten them well.

5 Cook over low heat for 2 minutes. Turn off the heat
and have a saucepan lid ready in case you need to put
out the flame. Pour the Cointreau and brandy over the
sauce without stirring. Immediately light the sauce with
a match, standing well back from the pan. Serve the
crêpes on warmed plates. Fresh vanilla ice cream is a
lovely accompaniment.

Chef's tip If you have any leftover crêpes, they can be
stacked, wrapped in foil and frozen in an airtight bag.
To defrost, simply refrigerate them overnight, then peel
off to use as needed.

Burgundy granita

A granita in Italian—or granité in French—is a close cousin to the true sorbet. It is made with sharp-tasting fruit, spiked with wine or champagne. Due to its low sugar content, small crystals form during freezing, giving the dessert its name: a granita should always give the impression of crushed ice.

Preparation time **10 minutes + 3 hours freezing**
Total cooking time **5 minutes**
Serves 8

3/4 cup sugar
1/3 cup orange juice
2 tablespoons lime juice
I tablespoon chopped lemon balm or mint
3 cups Burgundy or other red wine
sprigs of lemon balm or mint, to garnish

1 Chill eight serving glasses in the refrigerator. Place the sugar, orange juice, lime juice, lemon balm or mint and 1/2 cup water in a saucepan over medium heat. Ensuring the mixture doesn't boil, stir until the sugar dissolves. Bring to a boil, reduce the heat and simmer for 2–3 minutes.
2 Strain the syrup through a fine sieve, allow it to cool thoroughly, then add the wine. Stir well and pour the mixture into a shallow freezer container. Freeze for 3 hours, or until set.
3 When it is fully frozen and crystallized, scrape the granita into the chilled glasses using a metal spoon. Decorate each glass with sprigs of lemon balm or mint and serve at once.

Oeufs à la neige

In English, this amazing dessert is better known as "floating islands," or more literally "snow eggs." A rich custard sauce (crème anglaise) is topped with meltingly soft meringues and drizzled with caramel.

*Preparation time **40 minutes***
*Total cooking time **40 minutes***
Serves 6–8

✿ ✿ ✿

SYRUP
3/4 cup sugar

CREME ANGLAISE
2 cups milk
I vanilla bean
6 egg yolks
1/2 cup sugar

MERINGUES
6 egg whites
1/2 cup sugar

CARAMEL
1/3 cup sugar
lemon juice, to taste

1 To make the syrup, dissolve the sugar in 2 quarts water over low heat. Bring to a boil, then reduce the heat and leave to simmer gently.

2 To make the crème anglaise, prepare a large bowl of ice or iced water and place a smaller bowl inside. Put the milk and vanilla bean in a heavy-bottomed saucepan, and just bring to a boil. Make the custard using the Chef's techniques on page 63, then strain into the prepared bowl in the ice. Set aside to allow to cool, stirring occasionally.

3 To make the meringues, beat the egg whites in a clean, dry bowl until stiff peaks form. Add the sugar and beat until smooth and glossy. Shape into "eggs" using two large spoons dipped in water, then poach in the gently simmering syrup for 3 minutes; do not crowd the pan. Turn using a slotted spoon and poach for 3 more minutes. Drain on a dish towel, and set aside to cool.

4 To make the caramel sauce, place the sugar, 3 tablespoons water and a few drops of lemon juice in a heavy-bottomed saucepan. Stir over low heat until the sugar dissolves. Simmer for about 4–5 minutes, or until the caramel just turns a golden color: it should be thick and syrupy. Stop the cooking immediately by resting the saucepan in a large, heatproof bowl of iced water for a few seconds. Remove the saucepan and keep the caramel warm or it will harden.

5 To serve, fill a shallow serving bowl with crème anglaise and top with poached meringues. Drizzle the caramel over and serve the remainder on the side.

Baked apple and fruit charlotte

*As legend has it, this famous molded dessert was named after the wife of George III,
England's famous "mad" king. It is traditionally set in a tall, bucket-shaped mold.*

*Preparation time **30 minutes + 1 hour cooling***
*Total cooking time **1 hour 20 minutes***
Serves 6

14 thin slices of white bread, trimmed of crusts
3/4 cup unsalted butter
1 lb. Granny Smith apples, peeled, cored and finely
**   chopped (about 3 medium)**
1 lb. tart cooking apples, peeled, cored and finely
**   chopped (about 3 medium)**
1/2 cup lightly packed brown sugar
pinch of ground cinnamon
1/2 teaspoon ground nutmeg
1/2 cup finely chopped walnuts
1/3 cup golden raisins or mixed dried fruits
2 tablespoons marmalade (optional)
grated lemon rind (optional)
1/4 cup smooth jam (see Chef's tips)

1 Brush a 5-cup charlotte mold with softened butter.
Cut six slices of bread in half to form rectangles; cut five
slices in half at a diagonal to form triangles. Reserve the
remaining three slices of bread.

2 Turn the mold upside down and place the bread
triangles on top, overlapping the edges to completely
cover the top of the mold. Hold the triangles in place
and, using the mold as a guide, trim the excess edges
with scissors so the triangles will fit inside the base of
the mold exactly.

3 Melt 2/3 cup of the butter, dip the trimmed triangles
in, then line the base of the mold. Dip the rectangles in
butter and arrange around the sides, overlapping the
edges until the mold is completely covered, filling any
gaps with the bread trimmings. Dip the reserved slices
of bread in the butter and set aside.

4 To make the filling, melt the remaining butter in a
large skillet. Add the apples, cover the pan with
parchment paper and then a lid. Cook the apples over
low heat for 15–20 minutes, or until they are soft and of
the consistency of apple sauce. Add the brown sugar and
stir over high heat for about 5 minutes, or until the
mixture falls from the side of the spoon in wide drops.
Stir in the cinnamon, nutmeg, walnuts and raisins.
Remove from the heat. Add the marmalade, and
perhaps a little grated lemon rind. Set aside to cool.

5 Preheat the oven to 375°F. Ladle the filling into the
mold until half full. Cover the filling with half the
reserved bread slices, press down firmly, then add the
remaining filling. If the filling is not level with the mold
lining, trim the bread with the tip of a small knife or
scissors. Cover with the remaining reserved bread, filling
any gaps. Press in gently and cover with foil.

6 Place the charlotte on a baking sheet and bake for
45 minutes to 1 hour, or until golden and firm. Leave to
cool completely before turning out onto a serving plate:
this should take about 1 hour.

7 Warm the apricot jam and 2 tablespoons water in a
small saucepan over low heat until melted. Using a pastry
brush, brush the mixture over the surface of the charlotte
to give a light glaze.

Chef's tips A soufflé dish or a 4-inch-deep cake pan can
be used instead of a charlotte mold.

If the jam is very fruity, it will be easier to brush onto
the charlotte if it has been strained after warming.

For extra zest, you can replace the raisins with
1–2 tablespoons chopped candied ginger and the
nutmeg with ground ginger.

As an indulgent and luxurious accompaniment, whip
2/3 cup whipping cream with 2 tablespoons sugar, then
stir in 2 tablespoons of Calvados.

Gooseberry fool

England is the home of this old-fashioned but delicious dessert made of cooked, strained and puréed fruit, chilled and folded into custard and whipped cream. Traditionally, fool is made from gooseberries, although any fruit may be used.

*Preparation time **40 minutes + 2 hours refrigeration***
*Total cooking time **25 minutes***
Serves 4–6

✿

GOOSEBERRY PUREE
¹/₂ cup sugar
4 cups fresh gooseberries, trimmed at both ends
I leaf gelatin or ¹/₂ teaspoon gelatin powder

2 tablespoons cornstarch
¹/₄ cup sugar
¹/₂ cup milk
¹/₂ cup Greek or plain thick yogurt
¹/₄ cup whipping cream
I egg white
¹/₃ cup whipping cream, to serve
4–6 macaroons, to serve

1 To make the purée, reserve 1 tablespoon of sugar and place the rest in a heavy-bottomed saucepan with 1 cup water. Stir over low heat until the sugar dissolves. Bring to a boil, add the fruit, reduce the heat and simmer for 10 minutes, or until tender. Strain off the liquid. Purée the fruit in a food processor, then stir in the reserved sugar. Soak the gelatin leaf or powder, following the Chef's techniques on page 63.

2 In a separate heatproof bowl, combine the cornstarch and 1 tablespoon of the sugar. Add ¹/₄ cup of the milk and stir until smooth. Bring the remaining milk almost to a boil, then whisk it into the cornstarch and sugar. Place in a clean pan and whisk over low heat until the mixture boils and thickens. Remove from the heat.

3 Stir the soaked gelatin into the hot custard until dissolved, then cover with parchment paper and leave to cool. Stir in the fruit purée and yogurt, mixing well.

4 Whip the cream until soft peaks form, then fold into the custard. Whisk the egg white in a clean, dry bowl until stiff, then whisk in the remaining sugar and fold into the custard. Pipe or spoon the fool into tall glasses, ensuring there are no air pockets. Chill for 2 hours to set. Serve with freshly whipped cream and macaroons.

Chef's tip If the gooseberries are tart, sweeten them with a little sugar. Frozen gooseberries may be used in this recipe if fresh are not available.

Cabinet puddings

In this classic English dessert, leftover sponge cake is transformed into a scrumptious treat, often soaked in liqueur, dressed with dried fruit and custard, then baked in individual flower-pot shaped molds. Cabinet pudding is usually served with vanilla custard.

Preparation time 35 minutes
Total cooking time 1 hour 20 minutes
Serves 4

❁ ❁

sugar, for dusting
4 oz. sponge or chiffon cake
1 tablespoon chopped glacé cherries
2 tablespoons dried currants
1/4 cup golden raisins
1 tablespoon Kirsch
2 eggs
2 tablespoons sugar
1/2 teaspoon vanilla extract
1 cup milk

1 Preheat the oven to 300°F. Lightly brush four 2/3-cup dariole molds with softened butter. Place some sugar in a mold and, without placing your fingers inside the mold, rotate it so that a layer of sugar adheres to the butter. Tap out any excess sugar and repeat with the other molds.

2 Cut the sponge or chiffon cake into 1/4-inch cubes and mix in a bowl with the cherries, currants and raisins. Pour the Kirsch over, toss lightly, then leave to soak for a few minutes. Divide the cake and fruit mixture among the four molds.

3 Beat the eggs lightly in a large heatproof bowl and whisk in the sugar and vanilla. Warm the milk in a small, heavy-bottomed saucepan until bubbles show around the edge of the pan. Follow the method for making custard in the Chef's techniques on page 63, then pour the custard into each of the molds.

4 Half-fill a baking dish with hot water, place the molds in the dish and set aside for 5 minutes. Bake for 1 hour, or until the puddings are just firm to the light touch of a finger. Remove from the oven and cool for 3–4 minutes before turning out onto warm serving dishes. Serve with vanilla custard.

Chef's tips You can purchase a sponge or chiffon cake layer from your local bakery, or prepare one from a mix.

Look for dariole molds in gourmet cookware stores or use soufflé dishes or custard cups.

Gratin of fruits

Gratins are broiled until golden, giving a glorious, appetizing color. Here, a warm, rich sabayon provides a sensational topping to a simple medley of fresh summer fruit.

*Preparation time **30 minutes***
*Total cooking time **25–30 minutes***
Serves 4

2 peaches
2 nectarines
2 plums
4 litchi (lychee) nuts
2 passionfruit
1²/₃ cups strawberries
2 cups raspberries
2 eggs, plus 2 egg yolks
¹/₃ cup sugar
1 tablespoon Kirsch
fresh mint leaves, to decorate

1 Wash the peaches, nectarines and plums and dry them well. Cut the fruits in half, then twist the two halves in opposite directions to separate them. Remove the stones and thinly slice the fruits.

2 Peel away the tough brittle skin of the litchi (lychee) nuts. Slit each fruit down one side through to the stone, then open the flesh and remove the stone. Cut the passionfruit in half, scooping the pulp and seeds into a bowl. Rinse the strawberries and hull them. Arrange all the fruit decoratively on four heatproof plates or gratin dishes, then spoon the passionfruit pulp and seeds all over the top.

3 Place the eggs, yolks and sugar in the top of a double boiler, then place over a pan of barely simmering water. Whisk for 10–15 minutes, or until the mixture becomes thick and creamy and leaves a trail as it falls from the whisk. Stir in the Kirsch, then heat the broiler to a high setting.

4 Spoon the sauce over the fruit and broil quickly until the sabayon is an even brown. Decorate with mint leaves and serve.

Chef's tips The fruit plates can be prepared beforehand and covered with plastic wrap to prevent the fruit drying out.

If fresh litchi are not available, use canned, drained litchi which have already had their skins removed.

Apple fritters

The apples in this classic favorite can be replaced with almost any fruit that cooks well. Bananas, pineapple and pears are perfect substitutes.

Preparation time **35 minutes**
Total cooking time **20 minutes**
Serves 6–8

1³/4 lb. Golden Delicious apples (about 4–5)
1/2 cup sugar
1/3 cup Calvados or applejack
2¹/2 cups all-purpose flour
2¹/2 tablespoons cornstarch
2 eggs, plus 4 egg whites
1 cup beer
oil, for deep-frying
confectioners' sugar, for dusting

1 Peel and core the apples, then slice them into 1/2-inch thick rounds so that each has a hole in the center. Combine 1/3 cup of the sugar with the Calvados or applejack and use it to coat the apple. Set aside.

2 Sift the flour, cornstarch and a pinch of salt into a large bowl. Make a well in the center and whisk in the two eggs, the beer and then 1 tablespoon oil. Mix to a smooth, lump-free batter and set aside to rest. (The batter will be very thick, to coat and cook the apples.) Fill a large deep saucepan or deep-fryer one-third full with oil. Preheat to 325°F.

3 Beat the egg whites until soft peaks form, then add the remaining sugar. Beat until smooth and glossy. Fold into the batter with a large metal spoon.

4 Drain the apples on paper towels. Dip the slices in batter one at a time and deep-fry. Once browned, turn and cook the other side. Remove and drain on paper towels. Serve either warm or hot, sprinkled with confectioners' sugar.

Crêpes soufflés

An old French custom when cooking crêpes is to make a wish while flipping the crêpe, holding a coin in the hand for prosperity. Your guests will feel blessed indeed when offered this ambrosial dessert.

*Preparation time **40 minutes + 1 hour resting***
*Total cooking time **15 minutes***
Makes 9 crêpes

CREPE BATTER
2 tablespoons sugar
1/2 cup all-purpose flour
1 egg, lightly beaten
3/4 cup milk
1/4 teaspoon vanilla extract

unsalted butter, for cooking

SOUFFLE FILLING
1 cup milk
1/4 vanilla bean, split lengthwise
1/2 cup sugar
4 egg yolks
2 1/2 tablespoons cornstarch
1–2 teaspoons Grand Marnier
5 egg whites

1 To make the crêpes, sift the sugar, flour and a pinch of salt into a bowl. Make a well in the center and add the egg. Whisk briskly to blend in the flour, slowly adding half the milk in a thin steady stream. Whisk until smooth. Add the vanilla and remaining milk, whisking constantly into a smooth batter—you may need to strain the batter to remove all the lumps. Cover with plastic wrap and rest for at least 1 hour, preferably overnight.
2 Over medium heat, melt some butter in a 6-inch heavy-bottomed or nonstick crêpe pan; pour out any excess butter. Stir the batter well and pour into the pan from a ladle or pitcher, starting in the center and swirling the pan to create a thin layer. Cook for 1 minute, or until bubbles appear, the batter sets and the edges are brown. Carefully loosen and lift the edges with a palette knife or spatula. Turn and cook for 30 seconds, or until lightly golden. Remove from the pan with the first-fried side facing down. Set aside. Repeat with the remaining batter. When cooled, lightly sprinkle the crêpes with sugar and stack them, separated with parchment paper. Preheat the oven to 350°F.
3 To make the soufflé filling, slowly bring the milk and vanilla bean to a boil in a medium saucepan. Remove from the heat and set aside for 3 minutes to infuse the milk. In a separate bowl, vigorously beat the sugar and egg yolks with a wire whisk until pale. Stir in the cornstarch, gradually pour in the scalded milk and return the mixture to the pan. Stir for 2–3 minutes over moderate heat, or until thickened. Stir in the Grand Marnier, cover with parchment paper and set aside.
4 Remove the vanilla bean from the custard. In a separate bowl, whisk the egg whites until stiff peaks form. Using a large metal spoon, fold the egg whites into the custard in at least three batches. Gently fold until the mixture is well combined: it should be light and airy.
5 Place some filling on one half of the paler side of the crêpes. Fold over into a semicircle, but do not seal the edges. Place on a lightly greased baking sheet and bake for 10–15 minutes. The crêpes will open slightly. Using a wide spatula, carefully place each crêpe onto a warm serving plate. The crêpes may be served with a chocolate or fruit sauce, but are also delicious on their own.

Chef's tip If the first crêpes stick, the pan may not be hot enough. Always present crêpes with the first-cooked side facing outwards: it is more nicely browned with a lovely lace-like pattern.

Chef's techniques

Clarifying butter

Removing the water and solids from butter makes it less likely to burn. Ghee is a form of clarified butter.

To make about ⅓ cup clarified butter, cut 6 oz. butter into small cubes. Place in a small saucepan set into a larger pot of water over low heat. Melt the butter without stirring.

Remove the pan from the heat and allow to cool slightly. Skim the foam from the surface, being careful not to stir the butter.

Pour off the clear yellow liquid, being very careful to leave the milky sediment behind in the pan. Discard the sediment and store the clarified butter in an airtight container in the refrigerator.

Baking a pastry shell

Baking an unfilled pastry tart shell prevents the base becoming soggy during cooking.

After the pastry has been eased into the prepared pan, use a small ball of excess pastry to gently press the pastry into the sides of the pan to fill the fluted edges.

Use a rolling pin to trim the pastry edges. Gently but firmly roll across the top of the pan. Refrigerate for 10 minutes.

Pierce the pastry shell to allow steam to escape during baking. Line with crumpled waxed paper, fill with rice or dried beans and bake for the time specified in the recipe.

Remove the paper and the hot rice or beans. Discard the paper. The rice or beans can be stored and used over and over again after baking.

Making custard

Slow cooking and gentle heat are required to prevent the custard curdling.

Whisk the hot, infused milk or cream into the beaten eggs and sugar. Pour into a clean pan.

Stir gently over low heat with a wooden spoon for 10–15 minutes, or until the custard coats the back of the spoon and leaves a clear parting when a finger is drawn across. Do not boil, or the eggs will scramble.

Strain the warm custard through a fine sieve into a clean pitcher to remove any lumps.

Making a soufflé ridge

A successful soufflé has a high "cap" in the center, just like a traditional chef's cap.

Run your thumb around the inside of the soufflé dish. The ridge this creates will help the soufflé rise evenly.

Making Italian meringue

Close-textured and shiny, this meringue holds up well for up to two days without cooking.

Boil without stirring until the syrup reaches the soft-ball stage, 234–240°F. If you do not have a sugar thermometer, drop 1/4 teaspoon of the syrup into iced water: it should hold its shape but be soft when pressed.

In a large heatproof bowl, beat the egg whites into soft peaks, using a balloon whisk or electric mixer. Avoiding the whisk, add the hot syrup in a thin steady stream, beating constantly until thick and glossy. Beat until cold.

Using gelatin

Leaf gelatin has no flavor or color, gives a softer set than gelatin powder, and is easier to use.

Lower the leaves or sheets of gelatin into a bowl of cold water, adding each leaf separately to prevent sticking. Leave to soak for a few minutes, or until softened.

When the leaf is soft and pliable, carefully remove it and squeeze out any excess liquid. If you are using gelatin powder, dissolve each teaspoon of gelatin in 1 tablespoon of water, following the manufacturer's instructions.

First published in the United States in 1998 by Periplus Editions (HK) Ltd., with editorial offices at
153 Milk Street, Boston, Massachusetts 02109.

Murdoch Books and Le Cordon Bleu thank the 32 masterchefs of all the Le Cordon Bleu Schools, whose knowledge and
expertise have made this book possible, especially: Chef Cliche (MOF), Chef Terrien, Chef Boucheret, Chef Duchêne (MOF),
Chef Guillut, Chef Steneck, Paris; Chef Males, Chef Walsh, Chef Hardy, London; Chef Chantefort, Chef Bertin, Chef Jambert,
Chef Honda, Tokyo; Chef Salembien, Chef Boutin, Chef Harris, Sydney; Chef Lawes, Adelaide; Chef Guiet, Chef Denis, Ottawa.
Of the many people who helped the Chefs test each recipe, a special mention to David Welch and Allen Wertheim.
A very special acknowledgment to Directors Susan Eckstein, Great Britain, and Kathy Shaw, Paris, who have been responsible for
the coordination of the Le Cordon Bleu team throughout this series.

The Publisher and Le Cordon Bleu also wish to thank Carole Sweetnam for her help with this series.

First published in Australia in 1998 by Murdoch Books®

Managing Editor: Kay Halsey
Series Concept, Design and Art Direction: Juliet Cohen
Editors: Katri Hilden, Alison Moss
Food Director: Jody Vassallo
Food Editors: Lulu Grimes, Kerrie Ray, Tracy Rutherford
US Editor: Linda Venturoni Wilson
Designer: Michèle Lichtenberger
Photographer: Chris Jones
Food Stylist: Mary Harris
Food Preparation: Kerrie Ray
Chef's Techniques Photographer: Reg Morrison
Home Economists: Joanna Beaumont, Michelle Earl, Michelle Lawton, Toiva Longhurst, Kerrie Mullins, Kerrie Ray

Library of Congress catalog card number: 98-65442
ISBN 962-593-432-4

Front cover: Shortbread cookies with fresh cream and fruit.

Distributed in the United States by
Charles E. Tuttle Co., Inc.
RR1 Box 231-5
North Clarendon, VT 05759
Tel: (802) 773-8930
Fax: (802) 773-6993

Printed in Singapore

05 04 03 02 01 00 99 98 10 9 8 7 6 5 4 3 2 1

Important: Some of the recipes in this book may include raw eggs, which can cause salmonella poisoning.
Those who might be at risk from this (the elderly, pregnant women, young children and those suffering
from immune deficiency diseases) should check with their physicians before eating raw eggs.